Contents

SPELLING

Making plurals	2
Same but different	3
Shhh! Silent letters	4
Doubling letters	5
Prefixes and suffixes	6
Quick tips	7

PUNCTUATION

Stops and starts	8
? marks and ! marks	9
Apostrophes 1	10
Apostrophes 2	11
Direct speech	12

GRAMMAR

Nouns	13
Adjectives	14
Adjective clauses	15
Pronouns	16
Verbs	17
Adverbs	18
Adverb clauses	19
Writing sentences	20
Paragraphs	21

READING

Reading fiction	22
Looking for clues	23
Reading non-fiction	24
What do you think?	25
Using quotes	26

WRITING STORIES

Planning your writing	27
Writing a plot	28
Writing about people	29
Story settings	30
Story openings	31
The main characters	32
People talking	33
Story endings	34
Cliff hangers	35
Unexpected endings	36

WRITING NON-FICTION

Advertising	37
Re	38
	39
	40
	41
Newspaper reports	42
Instructions	43
Verb table	44
Planning sheet	45
Writing task 1	46
Writing task 2	47
Reading fiction	48
Reading non-fiction	50
Answers	52
Beyond the book	59
Notes on tests	60
My notes	62
My tricky words	63
Puzzle code grid	64

Making plurals

Plural means more than one.

Some words make their plurals by adding s – they're the easy ones!

Lots of words do other things.

Here are the rules:

plural	words	examples	comment
add s	lots	bike/bikes biscuit/biscuits	easy-peasy!
add es	if it ends in s, x, ch, sh	class/classes fox/foxes	the clue's at the end of the word
add ies	words ending in a consonant and y – drop the y and add ies.	pony/ponies city/cities	tricky!
add s	words ending in a vowel and y	boy/boys day/days	these words don't like the ies rule
add ves	words ending in f, and fe	wolf/wolves knife/knives	very tricky!
add s	musical words ending in o	cello/cellos, piano/pianos	musical easy-peasy
add es	other words ending in o	cargo/cargoes hero/heroes	don't forget the e
odd ones	some words don't follow any rule and you just have to learn them	child/children ox/oxen tooth/teeth	anybody's guess!

This will help...

If a word has an odd plural, it will tell you in a dictionary.

Try these

Use a dictionary to find the plurals of these rule-breaking words:

chief   cliff   dwarf   gulf   oaf

reef   roof   handkerchief

Puzzle code

Which is the correct plural of **wife**:

wives **(Y)**   wifes **(H)**   wifies **(M)**   *Write the letter in the grid on page 64.*

REMEMBER

Most words make their plurals by adding s or es. When you've written the word out, check it looks right.

Same but different

Same sound, different spelling.

I went over there to their place to see the sea!

Get it? Some words sound the same but:

• they are spelled differently

• they have different meanings.

These words are called homophones and you have to learn which is witch (oops!) which.

Here are some useful homophones.

there (a place)	their (belonging to them)	they're (they are)
were (past tense of are)	where (a place)	wear (to wear clothes)
write (use a pen)	right (correct)	
here (a place)	hear (to use your ears)	

Handwritten:
1) I saw two too.
2) It was raining when I reigned. *(reigned)*
3) I was allowed to shout aloud.
4) I did some sums.
5) Hi! My son can you see the sun?

This will help...

Getting the right hear / here is easy.
Hear has an ear in it!

Try these

Put each of these pairs of homophones in a sentence.
Use a dictionary to help you.

1	too	two	4	some	sum
2	rain	reign	5	sun	son
3	aloud	allowed			

REMEMBER

Write some sentences to help you remember – like this:

My writing was right.

Puzzle code

I can see an animal like a rabbit with long ears.
Is it a hair (R) or a hare (O)?

Write the letter in the grid on page 64.

Shhh! Silent letters

Some words have letters in them which make no sound. They're not much use, but you still have to put them in!

Some of these silent letters come at the beginning of a word.

silent k: knife   knives
know   knew   knowledge
knee   kneel

silent h: honest   honour
hour   hourly
heir   heiress

silent g: gnarled   gnash   gnome   gnat

silent w: write   wrote   written
wreck   wreckage
wrong   wrongful

silent b comes in the middle and at the end of words.

comb   dumb
plumb   plumber
bomb   bomber

Some of these silent letters come in the middle of a word.

silent e: dungeon   pigeon
omelette   surgeon

silent u: biscuit   honour   labour
mould   shoulder

silent g: campaign   foreign   reign

silent t: castle   listen   often

silent w: answer   sword

This will help...

When you learn these words, put the sound of the silent letter in like this:

s – w – ord

Try these

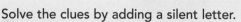

Solve the clues by adding a silent letter.

1 si**g**n: This shows you the way.
2 **w**rap   You do this to a parcel.
3 g**u**ess   You do this when you don't know the answer.
4 w**h**istle   You blow this.
5 **k**nob   You find this on a door.
6 lam**b**   A baby sheep.

Puzzle code

Which is the silent letter in **scissors**?

S (L)   R (O)   C (U)   *Write the letter in the grid on page 64.*

REMEMBER

Grouping words in families will help you remember the silent letter.

build /
builder /
building

Doubling letters

Learning the rules about when to double letters means you'll cut out lots of mistakes!

Here are the rules.

For most words which end in a short vowel and a single consonant, double the consonant before adding ing / er / ed, like this:

pat   patting   patted   **rub   rubbing   rubbed   rubber**

For most words which end in a long vowel and a consonant, or end in more than one consonant, don't double.

walk   walking   walked   walker   **wash   washing   washed   washer**

Be careful!

Words ending in a consonant and then 'y' are tricky.
You must change the 'y' to 'i' before you add 'er' or 'ed'.

carry   carried   carrier   **hurry   hurried**

Words which end in a vowel and 'y' keep the 'y'.

play   played   player

tip

Short vowels say their sound. Long vowels say their name.

This will help...

Look at the second to last letter of a word before adding ing / ed / er.

Try these

Add **ed** to these words.

hunt   laugh   carry   chop   walk
pat   shop   comb   hurry

hunted laughed carryed
Chopped walked
pated shopped
combed hurried

REMEMBER

Keep a list of the 'double trouble' words you use in your writing and learn them.

Puzzle code
Which of these is correct?

camping **(R)**   slaping **(F)**   jiged **(F)**   kicked **(R)**
campping **(F)**   slapping **(R)**   jigged **(R)**   kickked **(F)**

You should have answers all with the same letter – write this one in the grid on page 64.

On your toes   Add ed to marry.

Prefixes and suffixes

Prefixes

We can add letters to the beginning of a word –
that's a prefix.
Prefixes don't change the spelling, but they do
change the meaning! Sometimes a prefix makes
the word into its opposite.

Be careful!

If a prefix ends in the same letter as the
beginning of the word, you need both of them.

moral – immoral	satisfied – dissatisfied

Quick practice

You can make the opposite of these words by adding 'un' 'dis' or 'in'.

complete	trust	truthful	correct
like	sure	visible	kind

This will help...

The rule when adding a prefix is
'Just add it!'

Suffixes

We can add letters to the end of a word –
that's a suffix.
These are trickier as you have to watch your
spelling! Here are some useful rules.

- Adding **ly**: you can make adverbs by adding ly.

   silent – silently   stupid – stupidly

- The word **full** can be added to the end of
   words to make adjectives.

Be careful!

If the word ends in **l** you need both of them.

cool – coolly	beautiful – beautifully

If you want to add **ly** to words ending in **y** you
have to change the 'y' to 'i' first.

merry – merrily	happy – happily

Be careful!

You only need one l.

care – careful	thought – thoughtful

- **tion** and **sion** are useful suffixes.
   When a word ends in this sound, most of
   them are **tion** words.

   suggestion   attention

Most **sion** words are added to verbs which end
in 'd', 'de', 'se' and 't'.

persuade – persuasion   permit – permission

Try these

Add **ly** to these words:	Add **ful** to these words:	Add **tion** or sion to these words:
final*ly* ✓	plate *ful* ✓	describe*tion* ✓
actual*ly* ✓	colour *ful* ✓	pretend*sion*

REMEMBER

When you add a
suffix, think about
your spelling!

Puzzle code

Is the opposite of perfect

inperfect **(S)**   or   imperfect **(E)**?

*Write the letter in
the grid on page 64.*

Quick tips

ie or ei?

These words are a real nuisance but there is a neat way to remember!

i before **e** except after **c** but only when the sound is **'ee'**.

ee sound	ee sound after c	not an ee sound
achieve	ceiling	eight
chief	deceit	height
brief	receive	weight

This will help...
Learn the exceptions –
weird   seize   weir

Quick practice

ie or ei?

bel_ _f   conc_ _t   for_ _gn

g or j?

Many words sound as if they begin with **j** but, just to fool you, it's **g**.

If **g** makes a **j** sound then it is always followed by **i** or **e**.

hard g	soft g – says j
green	urgent
long	danger

This will help...
The letter **g** is used in many more words than the letter **j**.

Quick practice

Solve the clues with soft g words.

a huge person in fairy tales

a book has lots of these

a very small town

an animal with a very long neck

giant
pages
village
giraffe

c or s?

Some words sound like they have an **s** in them but – you guessed it – it's a **c** making a sound like an **s**.

If **c** makes an **s** sound then it is always followed by **i** or **e**.

hard c	soft c – like s
camp	certain
luck	since

Quick practice

Which looks right? danse or (dance)

REMEMBER

Learn these **ie** words:
brief   belief   chief
grief   thief
Keep a list of soft g words and learn them.
Collect soft c words and learn them.

Puzzle code
Which is the correct spelling?

shield **(E)** / sheild **(P)**

anjel **(P)** / angel **(E)**

sentre **(P)** / centre **(E)**

All your answers should have the the same letter. Write this letter in the grid on page 64.

Stops and starts

Capital letters **show where a sentence** begins.
Full stops **show where a sentence** ends.

Easy – but if you miss them out it makes life very hard for your reader.
When do they take a breath?

| **Read this:** | the boy came downstairs to have his breakfast he put on some toast the butter was hard the jam had gone mouldy he decided to have cereal instead |

This will help...

When you have added the capital letters and full stops, read it through. Does it make sense? Are you short of breath?

Still breathing?

Now, with capital letters and full stops it's so much easier to read!
Have a go.

The boy came downstairs to have his breakfast. He put on some toast. The butter was hard. The jam had gone mouldy. He decided to have cereal instead.

Capital letters have other uses, too. Special names need capital letters.

people's names:	Ivor Pain Eileen Dover
people's titles:	Mr / Mrs / Miss / Dr / Her Royal Highness
places:	Wobble Street / Leeds / Kent / Scotland
days:	Sunday / Monday . . . you know the rest
months:	January / February . . . when were you born?
book titles:	The Wind In The Willows . . . have you read it? It's very good!
organisations:	Tricky . . . but you know the sort of thing: e.g. shops – Plants Are Us, Tesco

Try these

Write:

1 • your best friend's name
2 • a book you have read
3 • your street or road
4 • the date of your birthday

① Harry Hugeus ② Batman
③ Victor Gardens
④ Delenber

REMEMBER

Always read through your writing and check for capital letters and full stops.

Puzzle code

Which one of these should have capital letters?

ant **(U)**   aberdeen **(V)**   apple **(M)**

Write the letter in the grid on page 64.

? marks and ! marks

Sentences always end with a full stop,
so what about question marks and exclamation marks?

The full stop is there in the question mark? and the exclamation mark!
Clever, eh?

Question marks show that a sentence is a question.

statement: You are wearing one shoe.

question: Why are you wearing one shoe?

This will help...

Think – does the sentence
need an answer?

Exclamation marks come after sentences
which show you that:

- someone is shouting or excited
- something very unusual has happened
- it's an order.

What's on your head?

Quick practice

Change the statements into questions.

You have a cat sitting on your head.

Sam doesn't like sprouts. *Does Sam like sprouts?*

> **There was a terrific rumbling noise and the volcano erupted!**

Try these

Add a full stop, question mark or exclamation mark.

They spent the night in the haunted house.
I'm going shopping today.
Get out of that muddy puddle!
Are you going out dressed like that?
I think I've won first prize!
What time is it?

REMEMBER

Every sentence must
have a full stop,
question mark or
exclamation mark.
Always read through
your work and check
you have put them in.

Puzzle code

What do you need on the end of this sentence?

*Write the letter in
the grid on page 64.*

Do you know what to do   . (F)   ? (E)   ! (W)

Apostrophes 1

We use apostrophes all the time when speaking because we run words together and make them shorter.

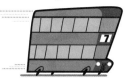

We've missed the bus!

He's in trouble now!

When you write these shortened words, you have to put in a mark called an apostrophe to show where you have left out letters. Words with apostrophes are called contractions.

The rule

Miss out letters – put in an apostrophe. It's easy!

The word 'not' is often used in contractions. Easy – it's always the 'o' that is missed out.

can not → can't

Quick practice

Match the words with their contraction.

words	contractions
they are	she's
she is	it's
I am	they're
it is	I'm

This will help...

Be careful! Will not becomes won't and shall not becomes shan't.

doesn't   isn't
can't   shouldn't x

Quick practice

Write the contractions for these 'not' words.

| does not | is not | can not | should not |

Life's never easy, is it? Sometimes a contraction has left out not just one letter but two. Don't worry. Do the same – put an apostrophe where the missing letters were.

he had → he'd

you've   we've   it'll   they've

REMEMBER

Try these

Write the contractions for these words.

you have   it will
we have   they have

Watch out for
I shall → I'll
and
we shall → we'll.

Three letters have been missed out here but still only one apostrophe is needed.

Puzzle code
Which is right?

must not → must'nt **(Y)** or mustn't **(N)**

Write the letter in the grid on page 64.

Apostrophes 2

Just when you think you've got the hang of apostrophes, there's a bit more!

The television's remote. The monkey's banana

The remote belongs to the

You also use an apostrophe to show that something is owned by or belongs to somebody or something. Are you following this?

Now read carefully!

Quick practice

Write these with an apostrophe.

the remote belonging to the television.

the banana belonging to the monkey.

1 When the owner is singular, add 's.

the coat belonging to the man

the man's coat

This will help...
Find the owner and add 's.

2 When the owner is plural and ends in s, just add '.

the desk belonging to the pupils

the pupils' desks

This will help...
Find the owner and put ' after the s.

The monkey's tails
the boy's football.

3 When the owner is plural and doesn't end in s, add 's.

the garden belonging to the children

the children's garden

This will help...
Find the owner and add 's.

boys'

Quick practice

Write these with apostrophes.

The tails belonging to the monkeys.

The football belonging to the boys.

The women's book shop   *The mouse's hole*

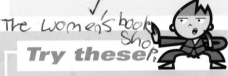

Try these!

Write these with apostrophes.

The bookshop belonging to the women.

The hole belonging to the mice.

REMEMBER

You can only add 's or ' to the owner.

Find the owner and you can't go wrong!

Puzzle code

Write the letter in the grid on page 64.

One girls' hands were dirty. **(P)**

or

One girl's hands were dirty. **(B)**

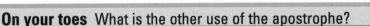

Direct speech

Direct speech is when characters in your stories are speaking to each other.

The rules

- Put speech marks around the spoken words.

  'Go away!' yelled Mary.

- Put punctuation inside the speech marks.

Now, there's one more thing to remember.

When a new person speaks you have to begin a new paragraph. You know, move your writing in a little from the margin.

This will help...

Remember that using direct speech in your stories makes them more interesting and you don't have to keep writing 'she said that' or 'he said that' all the time.

Bringing it altogether, it looks like this:

speech marks

punctuation

'We are going to miss the bus,' said Susan as she ran out of the door.

'Wait for me!,' yelled Barry. 'You can't go without me!'

'Do you want these sandwiches or not?' asked Mum as Barry hurried down the path.

'No time Mum. I'll just have to go hungry!'

Try these

Punctuate these direct speech sentences.
1 I've no idea how to play this game, complained Sam.
2 I've shown you, said Tom.
3 You'll have to show me again, said Sam. I didn't get it the first time.

Puzzle code

Which of the following is correctly punctuated?
'I like cats best,' sighed Gemma. **(E)**
Get out of my way right now" growled Luke. **(H)**

Write the letter in the grid on page 64.

REMEMBER

Remember – the speech marks go before and after the words that are actually spoken.

On your toes Write this as direct speech: The boy said that he was lost. *'I'm lost' said the boy.*

Nouns

All nouns are naming words but there are different kinds.

Common nouns

These are the names of ordinary, everyday things which you can touch, see or feel.

book   air   sky

floor   television

Proper nouns

These are the names of special things – remember, you did this when we looked at capital letters.

Carol   Manchester United

Sainsbury's   Friday

November   Mrs Dodd

Abstract nouns

These are tricky because you can't see or touch abstract nouns. They are the names of qualities and feelings.

beauty   silence

happiness

Collective nouns

These are the names of groups of things.

band (a few musicians)

orchestra (a lot of musicians)

unit (a few soldiers)

army (more soldiers)

This will help...

If you can put 'the' in front of the word, then it's a noun but you don't put 'the' in front of a proper noun.
- The **book** was on the floor.
- The **silence** in the room was strange.
- The **orchestra** played very badly.
- **Manchester United** won.

Nouns are much more interesting if you use adjectives as well, so read on.

Try these

The following nouns are in the wrong columns, which column should they be in?

common noun	proper noun	abstract noun	collective noun
tree	horror	Wilson Street	library
misery	Bob	shoal	computer

Puzzle code

What sort of animals go around in a group called a pride?

monkeys **(C)**   lions **(T)**   dogs **(I)**

Write the letter in the grid on page 64.

Adjectives

Adjective is the posh name for a describing word.

Adjectives are really useful as they make your writing much more interesting.

This is a plain, old, ordinary sentence:

> **The fox scrambled into its hole.**

> There's a fox and a hole. That's all you know.

Now look again.

> The **frightened** fox scrambled into its **secret** hole.

> So now you know how the fox was feeling and that no one else knew about the hole.

See – adjectives give you lots of interesting information.

This will help...

Look through your writing and find the nouns. Would they be more interesting if you added adjectives?

Quick practice

Add an interesting adjective to each of these nouns.

book   glove   meal   film

Adjectives help you compare things.

[handwritten: Comparisons more than two most incredible Most wonderfull happier harder]
[handwritten: Comparisons t... happy wonderfull hard incredible]

> **a big hole**   **a bigger hole**   **the biggest hole**

Short adjectives, like big, small, heavy, etc., use **er** when you are comparing two things and **est** when you are comparing more than two things.

Longer adjectives, like beautiful, frightened, etc., use **more** and **most**:

> *a beautiful picture*   *a **more** beautiful picture*   *the **most** beautiful picture*

Try these

Write these headings:
Comparison of two   Comparison of more than two

Now write the correct form of these adjectives under the headings:
happy   wonderful   hard   incredible

Puzzle code
Which is correct?   *Write the letters in the grid on page 64.*

terrible   terribler (Z)   terriblest (U)   or   most terrible (T)

REMEMBER

Don't use boring adjectives like nice and sad. Use interesting ones like marvellous or miserable.

Adjective clauses

Adjectives are great but if you really want to impress, try using a clause or two.

Adjective clauses **begin with** 'who', 'which' **or** 'that'.

They do the same job as adjectives, and make your writing even more interesting.

This is a plain, old, ordinary sentence.

They followed the path through the forest.

Now look again.

So there's a path and a forest. That's all you know.

This will help...

Adjective clauses describing *people* begin with 'who'.

Adjective clauses describing *things* or *animals* begin with 'which' or 'that'.

They followed the **uneven** path through the forest **which loomed menacingly on all sides.**

So now you know that the path was uneven (adjective) and that the forest was really creepy and threatening – that's what the adjective clause 'which loomed menacingly on all sides' tells you.

You can put an adjective clause in the middle of a sentence, but if you do, you need a comma before the clause and a comma after the clause.

Quick practice

Add adjective clauses to make these sentences more interesting.

The garden was bathed in moonlight . . . _which was covered by the shadow_ _The garden which was bathed in moonlight_

We watched the old man . . . _Who had a walking stick._

This will help...

You put the adjective clause inside commas so that if you take it out, you will still have a sentence.

The scooter, which Ed had won in a raffle, **had broken.**

Try these

Add adjective clauses in the middle of these sentences to make them more interesting. Don't forget your commas!

The newspaper, _Which I bought,_ was wet and torn.
My finger, _that I cut,_ was bleeding.

Puzzle code
Which is correct?

Write the letter in the grid on page 64.

The people, which . . .   The people, who . . .   The people, that . . .
(Y)   **(E)**   **(B)**

REMEMBER

Make sure you have a few adjective clauses in your stories to make them really interesting.

On your toes Would 'the dog' be followed by who or which?   _which_

Pronouns

Pronouns can stand in the place of nouns and prevent you repeating yourself.

The really useful pronouns are:

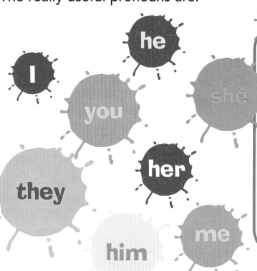

I he it you she her they him me

This will help...

The pronouns can be put into two groups.

doing the action	having the action done to it
I	me
he	him
she	her
we	us
they	them

The pronouns **it** and **you** don't change.

If we didn't have pronouns we would have to write like this:

> Nathan said that Nathan was going to visit Nathan's friend.

Pretty weird, eh?

Now, with pronouns we can write:

> Nathan said that he was going to visit his friend.

Much better!

Try these

Rewrite these sentences using pronouns.

The dog buried the dog's bone in the dog's favourite spot.

its
The dog buried the he's bone in his savourite spot.

Sally wanted Sally's sister to go with Sally to the shops.

Sally wanted her sister to g with her to the shops

The boys wanted to take the boys' bicycles with the boys.

The boys wanted to take there bicycles with them.
their

REMEMBER

Read through your story. If you have used a character's name too often, so it is boring, try using a few pronouns.

Puzzle code

Which do you think is correct?

Us marched all day. **(A)**   The army marched all day. **(R)**

Her marched all day. **(D)**

Write the letter in the grid on page 64.

Verbs

You remember every sentence has to have a capital letter and a full stop? Well, that's only half the story. Every sentence has to have an **action** word or a **being** word. These are called **verbs**.

Action **verbs say what something or someone is doing.**

One action verb you probably use a lot is said. However it's pretty boring. Here are some words you can use instead of said.

whispered   shouted   called   laughed
demanded   sobbed   shrieked
stammered   moaned   whined

The wind blew all night.
Henry stepped in a puddle.
The cat purred loudly.

Being **verbs tell us about something.**

The teacher was furious.   *This is part of the verb* to be.
I have a cold.   *This is part of the verb* to have.

Quick practice

Write the **action** verbs in these sentences.

The tiger (stalked) its prey.   *its* ✗

We (watched) the film again.   *the* ✗

Write the **being** verbs in these sentences.

Seb was tall and thin.   *was*

The farmer has thirteen cows.   *has*

The verb to be **and the verb** to have **can be tricky. The best thing to do is to learn them!**

Check out the verb table on page 44.

This will help...

Watch out for 'shall' which goes with 'I' and 'we', and will which you use with all the rest.

REMEMBER

Try to use powerful verbs in your writing.

Check that your sentences have an action verb or a being verb.

Puzzle code

For each pair, which one is correct?

I is	**(C)**	I am	**(A)**
He has	**(A)**	He have	**(C)**
They was	**(C)**	They were	**(A)**

You should have answers all with the same letter – write this one in the grid on page 64.

Adverbs

Remember how adjectives go with nouns and make them more interesting? Well, verbs have words which make them more interesting too. They're called adverbs.

Add to a verb = adverbs.

Adverbs tell you more about . . .

how **why** **when**

. . . things happen.

This is a plain, old, ordinary sentence.

The man was painting.

So, there's a man and he's painting. That's all you know.

- 'Carefully' is an adverb that tells you **how** he was painting.
- 'Here' is an adverb that tells you **where** he was painting.
- 'Today' is an adverb that tells you **when** he was painting.

This will help...

Look through your writing and find the verbs. Would they be more interesting if you added adverbs?

Now look again.

The man was painting **carefully here today.**

See – adverbs make verbs more interesting.

Try these

Write adverbs to go with each verb.

verb	how adverb	where adverb	when adverb
digging	quickly	Inside	today
climbing	cautiosly	here	yesterday
shouting	loudly	Outside	always

Puzzle code

Lots of **how** adverbs end in **ly** but you have to watch your spelling. Which are correct?

heavyly **(N)**   heavily **(T)**
merrily **(T)**   merryly **(N)**
shyly **(T)**   shily **(N)**

You should have answers all with the same letter – write this one in the grid on page 64.

REMEMBER

How adverbs are easy-peasy but where and when adverbs are more difficult to think of. Here are some useful ones.

where	when
here	today
there	yesterday
outside	tomorrow
inside	never
everywhere	always

Adverb clauses

Adverbs are great but if you really want to impress, try an adverb clause or two in your writing.

Adverb clauses are groups of words which begin with conjunctions such as:

because   when   if   although
unless   even if   even though

They do the same job as adverbs, only they make your writing even more interesting.

This is a plain, old, ordinary sentence.

The frog sank.

So, there's a frog and it sank. That's all you know.

Now look again.

The frog sank **because he was a terrible swimmer!**

So now you know that the frog was a terrible swimmer. And 'because he was a terrible swimmer' tells you why the frog sank.

Quick practice

Add adverb clauses to make these sentences more interesting.

It rained heavily _because it was a dull day_

The roof of the house caved in _even though the house had just been built_

This will help...

Adverb clauses often tell us 'why' something has happened or 'when' something happened.

So, does an adverb clause always have to come at the end of a sentence?

No way. You can put it at the beginning of a sentence, but watch out! If you do, you need a comma after the clause.

Even though she wasn't picked for the team, she still went to watch.

Try these

Add adverb clauses to the beginning of these sentences to make them more interesting. Don't forget your commas!

Even though I don't like beans, I like ice-cream.

Because you didn't do your work you can't go out.

REMEMBER

Make sure you have a few adverb clauses in your stories to make them really interesting.

Puzzle code

Which is correct?   _Write the letter in the grid on page 64._

Unless, you eat your sprouts you can't have any pudding. (M)

Unless you eat your sprouts, you can't have any pudding. (E)

Writing sentences

Now we've done capital letters, full stops, verbs and clauses
– all the things you need to know about to write really interesting sentences.
So, let's put it all together.

There are three main types of sentence.

1   A simple sentence with one main clause. A main clause makes sense on its own.

> The television was broken.

You can do these sorts of sentences in your sleep!

This will help...

> Use and when something is expected.
> Use but when it is unexpected.

2   A compound sentence is made up of two
main clauses joined by and or but.

> The television was broken and there was smoke coming out of it.
> The television was broken but we didn't care.

I trod on the cats tail and it sp at me.

3   A complex sentence is made up of two
or more clauses. One clause is a main
clause and the others are called
subordinate clauses. All that this means
is that they would not make a sentence
on their own.

Quick practice

Join these simple sentences to make compound sentences.
I trod on the cat's tail. It spat at me.
The food was disgusting. We ate it.

> The television was broken because he had knocked it over.
> The television, which was broken, was thrown out.

Tricky, but you'll get the hang of it with practice.

The good was disgusting but we at it.

This will help...

> Here are some useful words for joining subordinate
> clauses to main clauses to make interesting sentences.

conjunctions				pronouns
before	where	unless	until	who which that
because	so	although	while	
as	when	whenever	after	
if	even	though		

Try these

Finish these complex sentences.

There was an odd tree in the garden *so we pulled it down*

The match was really boring *so after the match we booed them*

REMEMBER

Don't always use
and and **but**.
Try and use
other conjunctions.

Puzzle code

Write the letter in the grid on page 64.

Is this a compound **(P)** or a complex **(N)** sentence?

Although I am not very good, I enjoy playing tennis.

Paragraphs

So, you have cracked sentences. Now, let's have a look at paragraphs. Sounds scary but it's dead simple.

A paragraph is a group of sentences about one main idea.

You need paragraphs in fiction (stories) and non-fiction (factual) writing.

This will help...

Think about time, setting and action.

Fiction

In story writing you can begin a new paragraph when:

• the time in the story has changed	Later that day . . . When the clock struck midnight . . . After several minutes . . .
• the place where the story is set has changed	In the garden . . . Further along the beach . . . On the other side of the mountain . . .
• the action of the story has changed	Sam began to scream . . . Suddenly, there was a loud explosion . . . The door creaked open . . .

Don't forget – begin a new paragraph when you are writing direct speech and a new person speaks.

Handwritten note:
• Later that day
• in the garden
• sam began to scream

Non-fiction

In non-fiction writing you begin a new paragraph when you write about different aspects of the topic. Suppose you are writing about lions.

paragraph 1:	what a lion looks like
paragraph 2:	where it lives
paragraph 3:	what it eats

Quick practice

Write a phrase that will begin a new paragraph when:

- the 'time' in your story has changed
- the 'setting' in your story has changed
- the 'action' in your story has changed.

Try these

If you had to write about your school what would you put in:

- the first paragraph *Where it is*
- the second paragraph *What it has*
- the third paragraph. *Whos who*

REMEMBER

Thinking about what is going in each paragraph is a good way to plan your writing. We'll do more about planning later.

Puzzle code

Is the 'action' of a story the plot (G) or the setting (H)?

Write the letter in the grid on page 64.

Reading fiction

Some of the questions in the reading test ask you to look for facts in a story or poem.

For questions like these, don't write what you think, and don't try to imagine what it feels like to be one of the characters.

These 'looking for facts' questions can be multiple choice. There are four possible answers to each question. Only one of them is correct. You should:

- **read the question and the possible answers carefully**
- **find the answer in the story**
- **put a ring around the correct answer.**

Look, it's easy . . .

Suppose you've read a story about Jack, the king's son, and the first question is:

a) Who was Jack?

the king   **the king's son**   **the giant**   **the giant's son**

So, you put a ring around 'the king's son'.

Some questions that ask you to find the facts are not multiple choice and you have to answer them in a different way.

Check out the space they give you for writing – that gives you a clue as to how much you should write!

You may have to:

- **write a word or phrase – not much room, just one line**
- **write a sentence or two – a few lines this time**
- **fill in a chart – big clue! They've drawn the chart for you!**

So, if the question looks like this:

Who was Jack? _____

You'll write: **'The king's son.'**

This will help...
These 'looking for facts' questions follow the order of the story so the answer to question 1 will be near the beginning, the answer to question 2 a bit further down, and so on.

REMEMBER

Don't be in a hurry! Read the story or poem and then read all the questions before you start scribbling.

Try these

'My name is Jo. I am a large black dog.'

What am I? What is my name?

A dog My name is Jo

Puzzle code

If 'comprehension' is the noun, what is the verb?

comprehensive **(M)**   comprehend **(L)**

Write the letter in the grid on page 64.

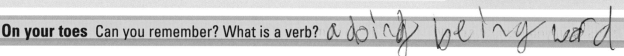

Looking for clues

What do you think?

As well as answering questions which ask for the facts from a story,
you'll also come across questions where the answers aren't written in the story.

So what do you think?

Look carefully at the questions. They might begin:

This will help...

Look at what a character says
and does to give you clues.

- How do you know . . .?

- Why do you think . . .?

- Explain why . . .

- Explain why you think that . . .

- Explain the reasons . . .

Now, you won't find the answers actually written in the story but, if you read
very carefully, you will find clues to help you. Let's have a go.

> **Tom ran into the shed and locked the door.**
> **He crouched down in the corner, not daring to make a sound.**

So, what do we think we know about Tom? He is obviously very frightened.

The writer hasn't used the words 'very frightened' but the clues tell us how he is feeling:

1st clue:	He runs.
2nd clue:	He locked the door.
3rd clue:	He crouched down to hide.
4th clue:	He stays absolutely still and quiet.

He doesn't sound like he's having a whale of a time, does it?

Try these

Read this part of a story and answer the questions.

> The day was overcast and grey. Kate stared out of
> the window and sighed. She wandered around the room,
> looking for something to do. It began to rain. Heavy, dark
> drops fell from the sky. 'Now that's ruined everything,' she thought.

How do you think Kate was feeling?

How do you know that what Kate was planning to do that day
was to take place outside?

REMEMBER

Read the question
carefully. It will
help you to decide
whether you are
looking for facts
or clues.

Puzzle code

Which of the following words means 'to think'?

wonder **(I)**   wander **(F)**

*Write the letter in
the grid on page 64.*

On your toes Can you remember? What's the plural of match?

23

Reading non-fiction

Some of the questions in the reading test ask you to look for facts in an explanation, a leaflet, a set of instructions, etc.
For questions like these, just read the passage carefully and find the answers.

These 'looking for facts' questions can be multiple choice.

There are four possible answers to each question. Only one of them is correct.

You should read the question and the possible answers carefully.

You should find the answer in the passage.

You should put a ring around the correct answer.

This will help...

These 'looking for facts' questions follow the order of the passage so the answer to question 1 will be near the beginning, the answer to question 2 a bit further down, and so on.

Look, it's easy . . .

Suppose you've read a passage about an extinct bird called the dodo and the first question is:

a) The dodo is:

a rare flower   an extinct bird
a precious stone   a fast car

So you put a ring around 'an extinct bird'.

Some questions that ask you to find the facts are not multiple choice and you have to answer them in a different way.

Check out the space they give you for writing the answer – that gives you a clue as to how much you should write!

You may have to:

• **write a word or phrase - not much room, just one line**

• **write a sentence or two - a few lines this time**

• **fill in a chart - big clue: they've drawn the chart for you!**

So, if the question looks like this:

What was a dodo?_____

You'll write: **'an extinct bird'**.   .

REMEMBER

**Don't be in a hurry!
Read the passage carefully and then read all the questions before you start scribbling.**

Puzzle code
Are stories normally 'fiction' **(S)** or 'non-fiction' **(J)**?

Write the letter in the grid on page 64.

What do you think?

As well as answering questions which ask for the facts from a non-fiction passage, you'll also come across questions where you are asked to explain something, pick out opinions and say why you think the text is arranged in a certain way.

So what do you do?

Look carefully at the questions. They might begin:

- **Explain why . . .**

- **How do you know . . .?**

- **Why do you think . . .?**

- **Explain the reasons . . .**

- **Explain why you think that . . .**

Now, you won't find the answers actually written in the story but, if you read very carefully, you will find **clues** to help you.

Let's have a go. Here is part of a passage about the planets.

We know far more about the Moon than we do about Mars. People have landed on the Moon, taken pictures and brought back rocks.

So, why do we **think** we know more about the Moon than Mars?

1st clue: People have landed on the Moon.
The passage doesn't say that people have not landed on Mars but it implies it.

2nd clue: We have close-up photos of the Moon. It doesn't say we don't have close-up photos of Mars but it implies it.

3rd clue: People have brought back Moon rock.
It doesn't say that we have no rocks from Mars but it implies it.

Try these

Read this passage and answer the questions.

It is quite easy to catch sight of a grey squirrel as they live in Britain in huge numbers. Seeing a red squirrel, however, is a different matter.

Why do you think it is difficult to see a red squirrel?

Puzzle code
Is 'brought' the past tense of

'to buy' (L)   or   **'to bring'** (H)?

Write the letter in the grid on page 64.

Read the question carefully. It will help you to decide whether you are looking for facts or clues.

On your toes Can you remember? Add ing to take.

25

Using quotes

It is useful to quote bits from the story or passage in your answer, but be careful!

Some questions ask you to find words and phrases from the story or passage.

This is easy! Just find the correct words and copy them carefully.

> Harry looked at his little brother covered in jelly and laughed loudly.

Question: What words in the story tell you that Harry thought what had happened to his brother was very funny?

Answer: He 'laughed loudly'.

This will help...

When you copy exact words and phrases, you put them in speech marks.

Quick practice

Read this and answer the questions.

> Kim and Barney climbed on to the Big Wheel and strapped themselves in. Kim waved excitedly to her mum and dad but Barney was white and shaking.

Which words tell you that Kim was enjoying herself?
Which words tell you that Barney was frightened?

Some questions ask you to answer in your own words.

You can still add some words from the story or passage to show where you got your answer from.

> Martin scratched his leg on the barbed wire and began to cry.

Question: In your own words, explain how Martin was feeling after he had scratched himself.

Answer: Martin was very upset. The passage says that he 'began to cry'.

Try these

Read this and answer the questions.

> The children shivered and huddled together for warmth. The torch light was fading and very soon it would go out.

Explain in your own words how you think the children were feeling.
Explain in your own words what was happening to the torch.

REMEMBER

Only put speech marks around the exact words you copy.

Puzzle code

'To explain' is a verb. Is 'explanation'
a collective noun (**O**) or
an abstract noun (**N**)?

Write the letter in the grid on page 64.

Planning your writing

Revise wise

You may be asked to write a story from a starting point.

Write a story which begins
with the sentence:
'I thought it was just going to be an
ordinary day like any other . . .'

Here's what you do

Look very carefully at your starting point.

Is it the title for a story?

Is it a sentence which you must use to begin or end your story?

Is it a brief description of a situation about which you can write your story?

Always keep your starting point in mind!

Now you need to plan your story

You will be given a planning sheet.
On your planning sheet, make brief notes about:

- **the plot** – what happens in the story

- **the characters** – who is in your story

- **the setting** – where and when does it happen.

This will help...

- Take no more than 10 minutes to plan your story. It's no good spending all your time on the plan. You won't get any marks for that!

- Write notes, words and phrases, not complete sentences. That takes up too much time.

- Just jot down some interesting words that you could use in your story.

- Remember to do this quickly – your planning notes will not be marked.

On the next few pages you will see the
bits of a story you need to plan!

REMEMBER

Plan carefully – you
need a beginning,
a middle and an end
– don't let your
story drift away
from your plan.

Puzzle code

What is the difference between a plan and a plot?
Is a plot:
key points about a story **(B)**   a series of events **(O)**?

Write the letter in the grid on page 64.

On your toes Can you remember? Is sadly an adjective or an adverb?

Writing a plot

The planning sheet can be used to make notes on:

- how your story begins
- what happens in the middle
- how your story ends.

We'll do some more about really great beginnings and endings later.

Here's what you do

Write these three headings on your planning sheet:

Beginning   **Middle**   **End**

This is going to help you think through exactly what happens in your story and will make sure you won't leave bits out or repeat yourself.

You need a beginning and an ending paragraph and you have to think about how many paragraphs you will need in the middle – a bit like making a sandwich, really.

Here are the plot planning notes for a story called 'Lost and found'.

Beginning:
mum, dad and child in town shopping
describe crowded street
child miserable

Middle:
child sees toy shop
mum gives dad shopping to take back to car
child wanders over to toy shop   (1 para)
mum realises child is missing
frantic search, asking people   (1 para)
dad returns
mum and dad continue search   (1 para)

End:
child bored with toy shop
looks round and sees mum and dad
goes back to them

This will help...

Try to plan the ending of your story before you begin writing. If you don't, you may find you don't know how to end and it will just sort of fizzle out! Not very impressive!

Try these

Write beginning, middle and end planning notes for the story on page 27:
'I thought it was going to be another ordinary day, like any other . . .'.

Puzzle code

Do you think **'frantic'** means 'relaxed' **(F)** or 'agitated' **(W)**?

Write the letter in the grid on page 64.

REMEMBER

Spending 10 minutes on your planning is not a waste of time! It will help you write a really good story rather than a muddle.

Writing about people

Revise wise

Characters are really important in a story.

- They have to be more than just names or your readers won't care about them.

- If your readers don't care about them, they won't care what happens to them.

- If they don't care what happens to them, they won't finish reading the story!

When you are planning you need to imagine each of your characters, so make notes on:

what sort of people they are

what they look like

their names

Here are the character planning notes for the story 'Lost and found'.

— Mum —
about 25
dark hair
quite slim
usually cheerful
tries to keep Ben happy

— Dad —
tall
same age as mum
light brown hair
impatient when shopping
– doesn't like it

— Ben —
about 5 years old
hates shopping
hates the crowds
curious
can be naughty

Try these

Remember the starting point you chose for your plot planning?
Use the same starting point and do some character planning.
Set out your notes like this.

Character 1: _____

Character 2: _____

Character 3: _____

This will help...

Don't have more than two or three characters in your story.
If you have more you can't describe them properly and they just become a list of names.

REMEMBER

Don't forget that characters in a story can be people or animals.

Puzzle code

Does the word **'personality'** mean
what someone looks like **(D)** or
what sort of person they are **(C)**? *Write the letter in the grid on page 64.*

Story settings

The planning sheet will ask you to think of a setting for your story.

Story setting   Where does it happen?

When does it happen?

You need to think about:

- words and phrases you can use for description
- how you want your readers to feel (frightened, curious, etc.)
- if your story has more than one setting.

Your reader needs to 'see' where and when your story takes place, as if you were showing them a photograph.

This will help...

Remember you can describe sounds and smells as well as what you see.

Here are the setting planning notes for the story 'Lost and found'.

scene	description	
A busy high street on Saturday afternoon.	*crowds*	jostling and bustling
	people	loaded down with shopping and carrying umbrellas
	noisy	people talking, laughing and getting cross
	weather	drizzling and damp
	time	late Saturday afternoon in winter
		shops with their lights on
		glistening puddles
	place	outside the toy shop with a colourful window display
		cuddly toys
		train going round

Try these

Remember the starting point you chose for your plot and character planning? Use the same starting point and make some notes about where and when the story is set. Set out your notes like this.

Scene   Description

_____   _____
_____   _____
_____   _____
_____   _____

REMEMBER

The setting includes time, place and the weather!

Puzzle code

'Description' is an abstract noun. What's the verb?

Describe **(O)**   Descript **(A)**

Write the letter in the grid on page 64.

Story openings

The **opening of your story** has to be 'attention-grabbing'.
It's no use if your readers are bored after the first couple of sentences.
You want them to read on, and on and on . . .

Paint a picture – take a photograph!

Not really, but if you decide to begin your story with a description of the setting then you are painting a picture or taking a photograph using words.

Look at these two story openings.

1 The castle was on the top of a hill. There was a moat around it. Further down was a forest.

2 The castle, dark and forbidding, stood on the hill, outlined against the fierce, orange sunset. The moat, which surrounded it, was filled with stagnant water over which a green slime had crept. The lower slopes of the hill were thickly wooded with stunted, gnarled trees that had formed themselves into hideous and frightening shapes.

This will help...

Read your setting description and ask yourself, 'Could I draw a picture from the details in this description?'

Opening 1   This doesn't really tell you anything much. There are no adjectives or adjective clauses so there is no description! You know there's a castle, a moat and a forest but you haven't a clue what they look like.

Opening 2   This is much better. You find out interesting details about the castle, the moat and the forest and you can begin to imagine what they look like. It also . . .

- leaves you with a creepy feeling – not a place you would probably want to hang around in for long

- starts to make you wonder what the story is about. Who lives in such an awful place? What horrible things are going to happen there?

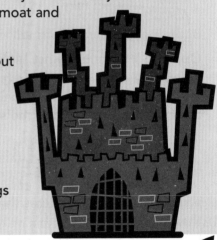

Try these

Write an opening paragraph to a story describing the setting of:

     a churchyard   a crowded swimming pool
        an empty football stadium

Puzzle code

Does 'stagnant' mean 'flowing' **(P)** or 'still' **(N)**?

Write the letter in the grid on page 64.

REMEMBER

Collect really good descriptive words and phrases used for settings from your reading and use them in your own stories.

The main characters

> Sometimes it's a good idea to introduce your readers to the main character right at the beginning of your story.

> It sounds quite easy but there's one way of doing it that is very boring and another way of doing it that's really clever.

Let's have a look . . .

You need to describe the character in detail and give the reader an idea of the sort of person that the character is. Here are two different ways of describing characters, which do you like best?

1 Mr Wilson was the man who saw the children of Blake Road School safely across the busy road. He always wore a white coat. He was quite fat and always cheerful. He liked children and they liked him.

2 Monday morning and the rain steadily poured down. Mr Wilson stood on the side of the road, a cheerful grin on his face and his white coat straining across his large stomach. He held his lollipop stick firmly in his right hand and waited for the children to arrive. For the next half an hour, Mr Wilson stopped the traffic to let the little ones cross safely, chatting to them about what they had done at the weekend and accepting offerings of sweets with a smile and a 'thank you'.

This will help...

> Read back over your character description and ask yourself, 'Have I simply written a list?'

Both opening paragraphs tell the reader about Mr Wilson.

Opening 1 describes what Mr Wilson looks like and the sort of person he is. Opening 2 does this too, but in a much more interesting way. Like the first opening, opening 2 lists the things the reader needs to know about Mr Wilson but it makes them part of the story and uses interesting phrases, such as:

'a cheerful grin on his face'

'his white coat straining across his large stomach'.

Writing in this way captures the readers' attention and makes them want to read on.

This will help...

> Always check your work for spelling mistakes.

Try these

Write an opening paragraph of a story describing the main character for one of the following stories:

The Martian   **The Stranger**   **Uncle Bill**

Puzzle code

Is 'Blake Road School' a common noun **(B)** or a proper noun **(G)**?

Write the letter in the grid on page 64.

REMEMBER

Collect really good descriptive words and phrases used for settings from your reading and use them in your own stories.

People talking

Get a conversation going!

An unusual way of beginning your story is to get your characters to start speaking to each other straightaway.

This is called dialogue. Your reader can get to know what sort of people your characters are by what they say and what one character says about another character.

Look at this story opening:

'I don't like this,' whispered Carl.

'Don't like what?' said Sam.

'I don't like crouching behind this wall in the dark. I'm cold and I want to go home.'

'Do be quiet!' hissed Gail. 'You'll scare the fox away before we've seen it.'

'Who cares about the stupid fox?' said Carl.

'I told you not to bring your little brother along,' snapped Gail. 'I knew he'd ruin everything.'

'Leave him alone,' mumbled Sam under his breath. 'You're always picking on him.'

'What did you say?' demanded Gail.

'Nothing,' said Sam.

'I want to go home!' wailed Carl.

This will help...

Direct speech needs:
- speech marks before and after spoken words
- punctuation after the last spoken word and before the speech marks
- a new paragraph when a new person speaks.

When **characters** speak to each other, you can find out a lot about them. From the dialogue in this passage we know that:

Carl	Sam	Gail
doesn't like being out in the dark	is Carl's older brother	is bossy
moans	is kind to his brother	is horrible to Carl
doesn't care about the fox	seems to be afraid of Gail	wants to see the fox

Here's a good tip: Don't always use 'said' in dialogue. There are more interesting words, such as whispered, shouted, snapped, whimpered, etc.

Try these

Write the opening paragraph of a story where two characters are speaking. Through what they say we have to tell which one is kind and which one is mean.

Puzzle code

Is the plural of fox foxs **(F)** or foxes **(R)**?   *Write the letter in the grid on page 64.*

On your toes Can you remember? Is it fense or fence?

33

Story endings

A good ending to a story is a must.

Nothing is worse than letting your story fizzle out like a damp squib.
If you don't think really carefully about the ending, you may find yourself
half way through, not knowing how to finish.

Imagine you have written the beginning and the middle of a story called 'Danger on the Cliff'.

*The beginning of the story is about two friends who go to the beach to have
a picnic. In the middle of the story the tide turns but they do not notice until
they are cut off and the only way to escape the water is to climb the cliff.*

How will the story end?

This will help...

> Always work out the
> ending of your story before
> you begin writing.

A happy ending

It's fine to have a happy ending for your story so long as you
don't make it too obvious at the beginning and in the middle
that everything is going to work out fine. Remember, you want
your reader to carry on reading until the very end.

Here's a happy ending for 'Danger on the cliff':

'We'll have to climb,' said Sean. 'We can't get back across the beach!'
Kim looked up at the sheer face of the cliff. 'I'll never make it.
I'll never get up there.' Her face was white with fear.
'We've no choice,' urged Sean. 'You go first. I'll be right behind you.
I'll help you.' Kim looked out over the vast expanse of water which
was already lapping at her feet. She began to climb, fear making her
fingers stiff and her legs like lead.
'You're doing fine,' Sean yelled from behind her. 'Just fine. Keep going.
We're nearly half way there!'
Suddenly, Kim's foot slipped. She let out a scream as she felt herself falling.
Sean grabbed her just in time and slowly they inched upwards and made it to the top.

Try these

Write a happy ending for a story where a character
has lost his or her dog.

REMEMBER

**Plan your story
ending carefully.**

Puzzle code

Is the plural of 'cliff'

'cliffes' **(L)** *or* 'cliffs' **(A)**?   *Write the letter in the grid on page 64.*

Cliff hangers

Not all stories have a happy ending where everything has worked out and the reader knows exactly what has happened.

Sometimes the ending of a story can leave you in suspense.

The story seems to stop suddenly and you don't know how things turn out. This is called a 'cliff hanger'.

How might 'Danger on the cliff' end with a cliff hanger? Sorry about the pun!

'We'll have to climb,' said Sean. 'We can't get back across the beach!'
Kim looked up at the sheer face of the cliff. 'I'll never make it.' I'll never get up there.' Her face was white with fear.
'We've no choice,' urged Sean. 'You go first. I'll be right behind you. Kim looked out over the vast expanse of water which was already lapping at her feet.
She began to climb, fear making her fingers stiff and her legs like lead.
'You're doing fine,' Sean yelled from behind her, 'Just fine. Keep going.
We're nearly half way there!'
Suddenly, Kim's foot slipped. She let out a scream as she felt herself falling.
Sean grabbed her just in time and pulled her to the safety of a small ledge.
They huddled there, getting their breath back.
'We have to keep going,' urged Sean gently.
'I can't . . . I can't!' sobbed Kim. 'I'll fall, I know I will.'
'Ok, Ok!' said Sean, realising that he was never going to persuade her to move from the ledge. 'Somebody will be missing us already. They'll come and find us, don't worry.'
He turned to look up at the top of the cliff.
'Or I'll have to go on and try to get help,' he mumbled under his breath.
'But I won't tell Kim, just yet.'

The reader is left wondering what will happen.
- Will somebody come and rescue them?
- Will Sean have to go on alone?
- Will he find help?
- Will Kim manage to cling on to the ledge?
- Will Sean be in time?

This will help...

A cliff hanger ending is not as easy as it looks. You can't just stop writing! You need to plan this type of ending very carefully.

Try these

You've written a happy ending for a story where a character loses his or her dog. Now write a cliff hanger ending.

Puzzle code
Does a cliff hanger create

suspension **(T)** or suspention **(V)**? *Write the letter in the grid on page 64.*

REMEMBER

A cliff hanger ending should leave your readers 'on the edge of their seats'!

Unexpected endings

Stories with an unexpected ending are sometimes described as having 'a twist in the tail'. This means that the ending is a complete surprise to the reader.

How might 'Danger on the cliff' end unexpectedly?

'We have to keep going,' urged Sean gently.

'I can't . . . I can't!' sobbed Kim. 'I'll fall, I know I will.'

'Ok, Ok!' said Sean, realising that he was never going to persuade her to move from the ledge.

'Somebody will be missing us already.' he said 'They'll come and find us. Don't worry.'

He turned to look up at the top of the cliff.

'Or I'll have to go on and try to get help,' he mumbled under his breath.

'But I won't tell Kim, just yet.' Suddenly, Kim stopped crying.

She rubbed her face on the sleeve of her jumper and said,

'This is stupid! I'm not going to stay here any longer!'

Sean watched in amazement as Kim began to climb.

Up and up she went, never looking down.

'Wait for me!' yelled Sean but he found he was too scared to move at all.

Kim, with one last huge effort, reached the top of the cliff.

She lay down and peered over, expecting to see Sean not far behind.

But he hadn't moved. 'Come on!' she yelled. 'It isn't that hard!'

'I can't move!' shouted Sean. 'You'll have to get help!'

Kim raced away to get help, leaving Sean to think what would happen when he was finally rescued. 'I'll never live this down!' he groaned to himself.

Unexpected endings are fun to write because you can have unusual things happening.

Who would have thought that it would be Kim who made it to the top and Sean who had to be rescued? Until almost the very end of the story we all thought it would be the other way around!

This will help...

An unexpected ending is not as easy as it looks. Don't rely on aliens landing from outer space every time!

Try these

You've written a happy ending and a cliff hanger ending for a story where a character loses his or her dog. Now write an unexpected ending.

REMEMBER

Don't always have an ending that the reader is expecting.

Puzzle code

Does an unexpected ending

suprise **(G)**   *or*   surprise **(U)**   your reader?

Write the letter in the grid on page 64.

---

36   **On your toes** Can you remember? Write I am cold in the past tense.

Advertising

Leaflets and brochures are a good example of writing to inform and persuade.

They are a type of advertising and they are designed to persuade the reader to visit somewhere, join something, buy something, etc.

What do you need to put in them?

- to inform: this is where you give your reader information
- to persuade: this is where you use vivid, exciting language to make your reader really interested.

This will help...

Make whatever you are advertising appear good value for money and really exciting.

You need to make a plan!

Information
Think carefully about the information your reader will need:

cost
opening times
facilities

Persuasion
Now this is where you really have to think carefully about the words you use.

Would you prefer to visit a castle that was described as:

nice   *or*   **an amazing journey into the past?**

Would you rather buy a pair of trainers that were described as:

smart   *or*   **fantastic?**

Would you prefer to go to see a film that was described as:

a bit scary   *or*   **a spin-chilling, hair-raising experience?**

See? The words you choose have to affect your readers and persuade them that they really must visit the castle, buy the trainers or see the film.

REMEMBER

Try these

Write three paragraphs to:
- **inform readers about a new swimming pool that has opened in your area**
- **persuade them to go there.**

Look at brochures and leaflets to see how they are set out and the sort of language they use.

Puzzle code
What is the noun from the verb 'to advertise'?

advertising **(P)**   or   advert **(L)** ?

Write the letter in the grid on page 64.

Personal letters

Well, we've done a lot about writing stories (fiction) but you're not finished yet! Now you have another piece of writing to do which is quite different.

This is a non-fiction piece and that can be just about anything, so get your thinking cap on and pay attention!

This type of writing could be a letter, a newspaper report, a set of instructions or an explanation.

You may have to inform your readers, persuade your readers or both! The purpose of the piece of writing will be made clear to you.

Let's start with a personal letter. These types of letters are fun. You send them to family and friends and you can write just about anything you like.

In a personal letter, you should always follow a few rules:

- Always put your address on the right hand side at the top, just in case the person you are writing to has accidentally (or on purpose!) lost it.

- Put the date on your letter under the address. Lots of people keep letters and like to look back and remember when they were written.

- Begin with Dear . . . (name of the person you are writing to).

- Begin the letter by asking how the person is, which is nice.

- Make most of the letter about why you are writing.

It may be to let the person know about something special that has happened to you, thank them for a birthday present or something like that, congratulate them if something good has happened to them, give them news about you and the family.

This will help...

Make sure your handwriting is easy to read!

- Write in a 'chatty style' just as if you were talking to the person.

- Remember your paragraphs. Begin a new one when you begin to write about a different subject.

- End a personal letter in one of many ways:

- Sign your name at the end.

See you soon
Best wishes
Lots of love

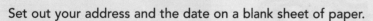

Try these

Set out your address and the date on a blank sheet of paper.

Puzzle code

What's another meaning for 'dear'?

expensive **(A)**   cheap **(N)**

Write the letter in the grid on page 64.

REMEMBER

Don't forget the date!

Write to a friend

This is how you set out a personal letter

5, Doodle Street, .
Markham,
Yorkshire
MA2 8AM   ← address

July 20th, 2002   ← date

dear... →

Dear Fred

friendly opening →

How are you? It seems ages since we went camping so I thought I'd write to see how you are doing.

I've been very busy revising for my SATs. I think I'm OK with Science and English but the Maths is a bit of a problem. I can't get the hang of some of it. How about you? Are you working hard?   ← **paragraphs for different subjects**

It was really great last week when the weather was hot. Mum and Dad took us to the beach and we had a fantastic time in the sea. Sam didn't like big waves but he's such a baby!

Well, I better get back to long division! If you have time, write and let me know what you have been doing. Have you got any new computer games?

informal ending →

See you soon

Ben

signature

This will help...

Try to write the sort of interesting, chatty letter that you would like to get.

Try these

Write a letter to a friend who lives a long way away, telling him / her about what you have been doing. You'll probably need some extra paper or it will be a very short letter!

REMEMBER

Don't forget your postcode!

Puzzle code

If 'signature' is the noun, what's the verb?

sign **(T)**   signate **(X)**   *Write the letter in the grid on page 64.*

Formal letters

These are also called business letters. You know, the type your mum or dad might write and receive.

Letters like this are written to request something make a complaint perhaps express an opinion.

In a formal **letter you should . . .**

- Write your address and date at the top on the right.

- Write the address of the recipient (that's a posh name for who you are writing to) a little lower down on the left.

- Begin your letter 'Dear' followed by the person's name if you know it:

  'Sir' (to a man whose name you don't know)

  'Madam' (to a woman whose name you don't know)

  'Sir or Madam' (if you don't know whether the person is a man or a woman)

- Use the first paragraph to explain briefly why you are writing.

- Use the following paragraphs to explain the details as clearly as possible.

- Use the final paragraph to explain what you hope will happen now that you have written – remember to make it clear that you expect a reply.

- Sign off with:

  Yours sincerely, (if you started the letter with the person's name)

  Yours faithfully, (if you started with Dear Sir or Dear Madam)

- Sign your name and then print it clearly underneath – just in case your signature is a bit of a scrawl.

This will help...

Write your letter in draft form on a piece of scrap paper – then copy it carefully.

REMEMBER

Don't forget to make your name and address clear – print them, just to make sure.

Try these

Write a letter to your local library asking when they are open.

Puzzle code

Is it correct to use yours sincerely (I) or yours faithfully (V) if you use the person's name?

Write the letter in the grid on page 64.

Business letters

This is how you set out a business letter

5, Doodle Street,
Markham,
Yorkshire
MA2 8AM ← your address

July 20th, 2002 ← date

Council Offices
12, The High Street
Markham
MA4 6BG

Who you are writing to →

Dear Sir or Madam,
I read the article in The Markham Daily News which said that there were plans to close the town's only park.

why you are writing →

I do not think this is a good idea as many children, including myself, use the park during the holidays. If you close the park, where will we play? I am sure you do not want children playing in the street near the traffic.

I know that many of my friends are also writing to you as they feel the same as I do. I hope you will think again about closing the park.

Yours faithfully,

signature → *Roy Brown*

printed name → Roy Brown

This will help...

Read through your letter. Have you made it very clear why you are writing?

Try these

Write a letter to the RSPCA. Explain that you are interested in the work they do and would like more information.

Puzzle code

Is the adverb from 'formal'

'formaly' **(J)** or 'formally' **(O)**? *Write the letter in the grid on page 64.*

REMEMBER

Read some of the letters printed in your local newspaper to help you see the sorts of things people write formal letters about.

Newspaper reports

Newspaper reports are written to inform the reader.

What do you need to think about in your planning?

- The headline – this is very important. If it's a boring headline then you won't grab your readers' attention and make them read on. It needs to be short and eye catching. Often reporters use alliteration, e.g.:

Scientists See Sea Serpent

- Sub-headings – these are useful for organising information in a logical way. They 'break up' the text and help the reader to follow the story.

- Eyewitness accounts – reporters often interview people involved in the story, so you are getting the information first hand, e.g.:

  Dr Dodd, a leading marine biologist, said, 'I've never seen anything like it before. It was huge.'

- Opinions – in a newspaper report people often have different opinions and you need to make sure that you include those opinions and do not 'take sides', e.g.:

  Many scientists think the serpent is a living relative of the dinosaurs, whilst others believe it to be a hoax.

- Your audience – you are writing for a wide variety of people, so your report should be clear and easy to follow.

This will help...

Check that your newspaper report answers the following questions:

Who?   What?   When?
Where?   Why?   How?

Organise your report like this

- The first paragraph should contain the most important information.
- The main part of the report should give extra detail, maybe an eyewitness account.
- The end of the report should contain the least important details so that, if you run out of space, it can be cut.

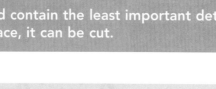

Try these

Write a newspaper report about a large animal escaping from the local zoo.

Puzzle code

If a biologist studies biology, what does a chemist study?

chemology **(R)**   or   chemistry **(N)**?   *Write the letter in the grid on page 64.*

REMEMBER

Read some newspaper reports to help you understand how they are written.

Instructions

Instructions are written to tell you how to do things, so if they are muddled and difficult to follow, they are not much use.

Things to remember when you write instructions:

- You need a title that shows what the outcome will be. In other words, what are these instruction for? For example:

 How to make an omelette   How to build your garden pond

- You need a list of equipment / ingredients:

You will need:

a screwdriver

a hammer

a tape measure

You will need:

6oz flour

3 eggs

a little milk

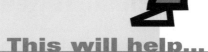
This will help...
When you are asked to write instructions, imagine that you are doing the task. Make a planning list of the things you must do, in the correct order.

- Long, complicated sentences are good for descriptive writing but you don't need them here. Keep it short and simple:

    Break the eggs into a bowl.

- You need to use very precise language:

    It's no good writing,   'Dig a big hole in the garden.'

    You need to be precise: 'Dig a 2 metre square hole in the garden.'

- It is always a good idea to number your instructions and make sure they are in the correct order!

    1 Break the eggs into a bowl.

    2 Add the milk and whisk.

- Now comes the 'technical' bit. Verbs in instructions should be imperatives. All that this means is that you write them as if they are giving an order:

    Don't write,   'You must put oil in the frying pan.'

    Write: 'Put oil in the frying pan.'

REMEMBER
Look at some recipes, rules for games, etc. and see if you think the instructions are clear and well written.

Try these

Write a list of clear instructions for preparing a bowl of cereal or recording a TV programme on a video tape.

Puzzle code
Which is correct:

Peel **(S)** the carrots or peal **(T)** the carrots.   *Write the letter in the grid on page 64.*

Verb table

To be

present tense – singular	past tense – singular	future tense – singular
I am	I was	I shall
you are	you were	you will
he / she / it is	he / she / it was	he / she / it will
present tense – plural	**past tense – plural**	**future tense – plural**
we are	we were	we shall
you are	you were	you will
they are	they were	they will

To have

present tense – singular	past tense – singular	future tense – singular
I have	I had	I shall have
you have	you had	you will have
he / she / it has	he / she / it had	he / she / it will have
present tense – plural	**past tense – plural**	**future tense – plural**
we have	we had	we shall have
you have	you had	you will have
they have	they had	they will have

Planning sheet

Remember to think about:

- how to start your story;
- the most important events in your story;
- how to end your story

This is for **very brief notes** to help you plan your story.

This will help...

Your notes will not be marked.

the plot

characters involved

details of setting

Magic Monday

It was an ordinary Monday – until the magic started!

Write a story based on this idea.

Allow yourself 45 minutes including your planning time.

Plan your story

Answering these questions will help you plan your story:

Who are the characters in your story?

How does the story start?

What is the magic?

How does it change things?

How does your story end?

Imagine you were in the classroom on that 'Magic Monday'.

Write a letter explaining what happened.

Remember . . .

Set out your letter correctly:

your address

    the date

        Dear . . .

           sign off.

Begin by expaining why you are writing.

Explain what happened.

Explain how you felt.

Reading fiction

Read the beginning of this story carefully and look
for clues to help you answer the questions opposite.

> The number of lines
> after the question
> gives you a clue about
> how much to write.

'Too many!' James shouted, and slammed the
the door door behind him.

'What?' said **Will**.

'Too many kids in this family, that's what. Just too many.'

James stood fuming on the landing like a small angry locomotive, then
stumped across to the window-seat and stared out at the garden. **Will**
put aside his book and pulled up his legs to make room. 'I could hear all the yelling,'
he said, chin on knees.

'Wasn't anything,' James said. 'Just stupid Barbara again. Bossing. Pick up this,
don't touch that. And Mary joining in, twitter twitter twitter. You'd think this
house was big enough, but there's always people.'

They both looked out of the window. The snow lay thin and apologetic over the
world. That wide grey sweep was the lawn, with the straggling trees of the orchard
still dark beyond; the white squares were the roofs of the garage, the old barn, the
rabbit hutches, the chicken coops. Further back there were only the flat fields of
Dawson's Farm, dimly white-striped. All the broad sky was grey, full of more snow
that refused to fall. There was no colour anywhere.

'Four days to Christmas,' **Will** said. 'I wish it would snow properly.'

'And it's your birthday tomorrow.'

'Mmm.' He had been going to say that too, but it would
have been too much like a reminder. And the gift he
most wished for on his birthday was something nobody
could give him: it was snow, beautiful, deep, blanketing
snow, and it never came.

At least this year there was the grey sprinkle, better
than nothing.

From *The Dark is Rising* by Susan Cooper

A In the first sentence of the story what two things does James do that show he is angry?

_____

B What sort of person do you think Barbara is?

_____

_____

C What impression do you get of Mary when James says 'twitter twitter twitter'?

_____

_____

_____

D Tick which of the following you think best describes James and explain the reasons for your choice:

i) likes to be with a crowd

ii) likes to be on his own

_____

_____

_____

E Will had been going to say that it was his birthday tomorrow but 'it would have been too much like a reminder'.

What does this tell you about the sort of person Will is?

_____

_____

_____

F Why do you think Will wanted snow for his birthday?

_____

_____

_____

Reading non-fiction

This information passage has both multiple choice questions and answers you must write yourself.

Remember, you may have to:

- ring the correct answer
- write words, phrases or sentences
- fill in a chart

You'll find all the answers in the passage.

Read this information passage carefully. Then read all the questions.
Go back and answer the questions, always checking in the passage.

Otters

Otters can be found near the coast among the rocks.

They also live in freshwater rivers and canals where there are enough bushes and trees to provide cover.

The otter is a very shy creature which comes out at night to hunt. It mainly eats fish of all types but its favourite is the eel. It will also eats birds, frogs and even baby rabbits.

Many years ago otters were hunted for their fur, or just for sport. They were seen as pests and people wanted to get rid of them. Despite this, otters continued to live in large numbers in this country until the late 1950s. By this time pesticides were widely used and much of the water which was home to the otters was polluted.

In 1981, a law was passed which protects otters as an endangered species.

Otter facts

An otter's lifespan is about 9 to 10 years.

A new born otter is blind and weighs about 60 grams.

When an otter swims underwater its eyes are open but its ears and nose are closed.

The long stiff hairs on the otter's coat are covered in oil to repel water.

You are most likely to see otters in Scotland or Ireland.

Young otters learn to swim at about 12 weeks.

An otter can swim underwater for at least 400 metres without coming up for air

a) As an otter dives underwater its:

ears and eyes close	ears and nose close	eyes and nose close	ears, eyes and nose close

b) 1981 was an important year for otters because:

people wanted to get rid of them	pesticides were used	young otters learnt to swim	a law was passed to protect them

c) Write down two reasons given in the passage which explain why otters were hunted.

i) _____

ii) _____

d) Explain in your own words why the number of otters went down in the late 1950s.

e) Using the information in the passage, write as many facts under each heading as you can to complete the chart. You should write notes, not sentences.

habitat (where otters live)	food	young otters

Have you answered all the questions?

Answers

SPELLING

Making plurals
Page 2

Try these
- chiefs
- cliffs
- dwarfs
- gulfs
- oafs
- reefs
- roofs
- handkerchiefs

Puzzle code wives
On your toes feet

Same but different
Page 3

Puzzle code hare
On your toes pear

Shh! Silent letters
Page 4

Try these
- sign
- wrap
- guess
- whistle
- knob
- lamb

Puzzle code C
On your toes e.g. fasten

Doubling letters
Page 5

Try these
- hunted
- laughed
- carried
- chopped
- walked
- patted
- shopped
- combed
- hurried

Puzzle code
- camping
- slapping
- jigged
- kicked

On your toes married

Prefixes and suffixes
Page 6

Prefixes
Quick practice
- incomplete
- distrust
- untruthful
- incorrect
- dislike / unlike
- unsure
- invisible
- unkind

Suffixes
Try these
- finally
- actually
- plateful
- colourful
- description
- pretension

Puzzle code imperfect
On your toes invasion

Quick tips
Page 7

Quick practice belief
conceit
foreign
giant
pages
village
giraffe

Quick practice dance

Puzzle code shield
angel
centre
On your toes e.g. accident
circus

PUNCTUATION

Stops and starts
Page 8

Puzzle code Aberdeen
On your toes August

? marks and ! marks
Page 9

Quick practice Why do you have a cat
sitting on your head?
Does Sam like sprouts?
Try these They spent the night in

the haunted house!
I'm going shopping
today.
Get out of that muddy
puddle!
Are you going out
dressed like that?
I think I've won first
prize!
What time is it?
Puzzle code ?
On your toes What time is it?

Apostrophes 1
Page 10

Quick practice they are – they're
she is – she's
I am – I'm
it is – it's

doesn't
isn't
can't
shouldn't

Try these you've
we've
it'll
they've

Puzzle code mustn't
On your toes let's

Apostrophes 2
Page 11

Quick practice the television's remote
the monkey's banana
the monkeys' tails

Try these	the boys' football the women's bookshop the mice's hole
Puzzle code	One girl's hands were dirty.
On your toes	contractions

Direct speech
Page 12

Try this	'I've no idea how to play this game,' complained Sam. 'I've shown you,' said Tom. 'You'll have to show me again,' said Sam. 'I didn't get it the first time.'
Puzzle code	'I like cats best,' sighed Gemma.
On your toes	'I am lost,' said the boy.

GRAMMAR

Nouns
Page 13

Try these

common	*proper*	*abstract*	*collective*
tree	Bob	misery	shoal
computer	Wilson Street	horror	library

Puzzle code	lions
On your toes	misery

Adjectives
Page 14

Try these

happy	happier	happiest
wonderful	more wonderful	most wonderful
hard	harder	hardest
incredible	more incredible	most incredible

Puzzle code	most terrible
On your toes	more frightening

Adjective clauses
Page 15

Puzzle code	The people, who . . .
On your toes	which

Pronouns
Page 16

Try these	The dog buried its bone in its favourite spot. Sally wanted her sister to go with her to the shops. The boys wanted to take their bicycles with them.
Puzzle code	The army marched all day.
On your toes	its

Verbs

Page 17

Quick practice stalked
watched
was
has

Puzzle code I am
he has
they were

On your toes I will be

Adverbs

Page 18

Puzzle code heavily
merrily
shyly

On your toes when

Adverb clauses

Page 19

Puzzle code Unless you eat your sprouts, you can't have any pudding.

On your toes when I've eaten

Writing sentences

Page 20

Quick practice I trod on the cat's tail and it spat at me.
The food was disgusting but we ate it.

Puzzle code complex sentence

On your toes e.g. where, when, while whenever

Paragraphs

Page 21

Puzzle code plot

On your toes e.g. autograph telegraph

READING

Reading fiction

Page 22

Try these A dog
My name is Jo.

Puzzle code comprehend

On your toes a doing or being word

Looking for clues

Page 23

Try these I think Kate was bored and rather fed up.
I know what Kate was planning was going to happen outside because, when it began to rain, Kate thought that everything was ruined.

Puzzle code wonder

On your toes matches

Reading non-fiction
Page 24

Puzzle code   fiction
On your toes   abstract noun

What do you think?
Page 25

Try this   I think it is difficult to see a red squirrel because the passage implies that there are far fewer red squirrels than grey squirrels.

Puzzle code   to bring
On your toes   taking

Using quotes
Page 26

Quick practice 'waved excitedly'
                 'white and shaking'

Try these   I think that the children were cold and probably frightened as it says, 'The children shivered and huddled together for warmth.'

The torch battery was nearly exhausted as it says it 'the torch light was fading and very soon it would go out'.

Puzzle code   abstract noun
On your toes   wasn't

WRITING STORIES

Planning your writing
Page 27

Puzzle code   a series of events
On your toes   adverb

Writing a plot
Page 28

Puzzle code   agitated
On your toes   dishonest

Writing about people
Page 29

Puzzle code   what sort of person they are
On your toes   k

Story settings
Page 30

Puzzle code   describe
On your toes   chief

Story openings
Page 31

Puzzle code   still
On your toes   pianos

The main characters
Page 32

Puzzle code   proper noun
On your toes   verb

People talking

Page 33

Puzzle code	foxes
On your toes	fence

Write to a friend

Page 39

Puzzle code	sign
On your toes	how

Story endings

Page 34

Puzzle code	cliffs
On your toes	they'll

Formal letters

Page 40

Puzzle code	yours sincerely
On your toes	children

Cliff hangers

Page 35

Puzzle code	suspension
On your toes	screamed

Business letters

Page 41

Puzzle code	formally
On your toes	witch's hat

Unexpected endings

Page 36

Puzzle code	surprise
On your toes	I was cold

Newspaper reports

Page 42

Puzzle code	chemistry
On your toes	improbable

Advertising

Page 37

Puzzle code	advert
On your toes	slipped

Instructions

Page 43

Puzzle code	peel
On your toes	dangerous

WRITING NON-FICTION

Personal letters

Page 38

Puzzle code	expensive
On your toes	differently

ANSWERS TO FICTION READING

(a) James shouted and slammed the door

(b) Barbara appears to be the sort of person who likes to be in charge and tell everyone what to do.

(c) The word "twitter" gives the impression that Mary fusses and goes on and on about things.

(d) Likes to be on his own. The clues in the story are that James thinks there are too many kids in the family/too many people in the house. Having people around makes him angry.

(e) Will is not the sort of person who goes around reminding everyone it is his birthday to make sure they buy him presents.

(f) The child should draw on his/her own experience to answer this question, e.g. perhaps he wanted to play in the snow, build snowmen, have snowball fights, etc.

ANSWERS TO NON-FICTION READING

(a) As an otter dives underwater its ears and nose close.

(b) 1981 was an important year for otters because a law was passes to protect them.

(c) Any two of the following: for fur/as sport/because they were considered pests.

(d) The answer should indicate that the use of pesticides infected the water where the otters lived, so many otters died.

(e) **Habitat**

near rocky coast
rivers and canals
with bushes and trees

Food

fish
favourite is eel
baby rabbits
birds
frogs

Young otters

blind when born
swim at 12 weeks
weigh about 60 grams

Beyond the book

10 tasks to help your literary skills

1   Join your school or local library.
    Borrow fiction and non-fiction books.

2   Keep a reading journal. Write the title and
    author of the book and what you thought of it.

3   Keep a diary. It's great fun looking back and reading it when you are
    older. Remember to write how you felt at the time as well as what
    happened.

4   Follow the instructions in a recipe book and make something good to eat.

5   Look at a TV magazine which gives you programmes for the week. Pick
    out your favourites and make a 'Best night on TV' page.

6   Make a 'Must remember list' which helps you remember the things you
    need to take to school each day.

7   Have a 'Best thing...worst thing' book. Write the best thing
    that happened to you each week and the worst thing!

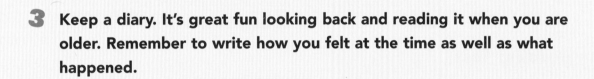

8   Write directions from your house to the school.

9   Read about interesting things which are happening in your area in your
    local newspaper.

10 Make your own dictionary. Collect interesting and unusual words which
    you could use in your own writing.

Notes on tests

About the KS2 English Tests

This book gives you lots of practice for the KS2 English tests but what exactly do you have to do in the test?

The first thing to say is that you've done it all before! You will be tested on the sort of English work that you have been doing at school for ages.

There are three parts to the English Test - a Reading Test, a Writing Test and a Spelling Test. Usually the Reading and Spelling test are taken on the same day, and the Writing Test on another day of the same week.

Your handwriting will be assessed as part of your Writing Test, with marks awarded for your 'best' section of handwriting.

The Reading Test

You will be given a Reading Booklet and a Reading Answer Booklet. You will have fifteen minutes to read through the booklet. It will contain a mixture of different types of writing, both fiction and non-fiction. There may be:

A short story   a poem   information   a letter   an interview

It is a good idea to skim through it and then read it more carefully section by section.

When the fifteen mintues are up, your teacher will ask you to write your name and school on the front of the Reading Answer Booklet. It has questions about what you have just read and you'll have 45 minutes to answer them. The teacher will explain that there are different types of questions to answer:

There's lots of practice for this on pages 48–51.

Multiple choice: there are several answers and you need to put a ring around the correct one.

Longer, detailed answers: need a few sentences explaining an opinion or idea.

Longer answers: need a sentence or two – there will be a few lines to write on.

Your teacher will remind you of the time halfway through the Test and 15 minutes before the end.

Tips

- Don't spend too long on any one question.

- If you find a question difficult, leave it and go back to it at the end.

- Don't waste time rubbing things out. Cross out neatly.

- You won't get marks if you don't write anything, so try to answer every question.

The Writing Test

There are two writing tasks. One is a longer piece lasting about 45 mintues, and the second is shorter lasting 20 minutes. There is a helpful planning sheet for each writing task. The tasks may be fiction or non-fiction or a mixture. You will have a break between the two tasks. Your teacher will remind you of how much time you have left as you complete the tasks.

Tips

- Try to leave yourself time to check what you've written

- You may use a dictionary, but don't waste time looking up lots of words – there are no marks for spelling in this test.

- Check your punctuation (full stops, commas, question marks, inverted commas and apostrophes), if you want to gain extra marks.

The Spelling Test

You will get a booklet which has a few paragraphs of writing in it. Some of the words are missing and there is a line instead, where you will write the words yourself. Your teacher read out the paragraphs, saying the missing words. Don't write yet, just listen carefully.

When your teacher reads the paragraphs a second time, he or she will pause after each missing word to give you time sto write it in the correct place.

Your teacher will read it out once more so you can check your answers and fill in the gaps.

- If you don't write a missing word in, put a little cross on that line so that you don't write the next word in the wrong space.

My notes

Use this page to make your own revision notes and timetable.

My tricky words

Use this page to remind yourself of those words
you find harder to spell.

Revise wise

As you use this book, work out the correct answer to the puzzle code questions on each page.

Write the corresponding letter in the right spaces below, to figure out the code.

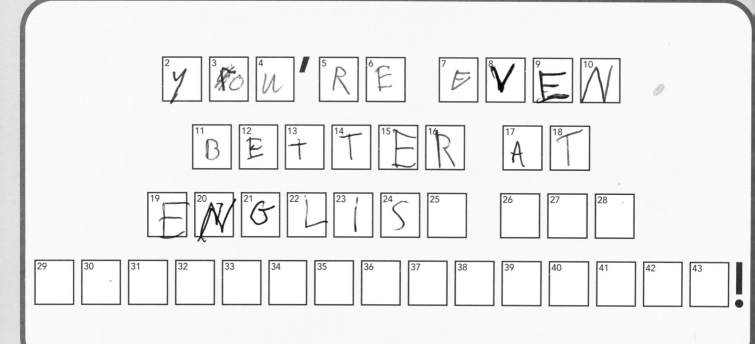

YOU'RE EVEN BETTER AT ENGLIS